To

From

Date

A FEARLESS LEADER

A BIBLE STORY ABOUT DEBORAH

RACHEL SPIER WEAVER · ANNA HAGGARD

Illustrated by ERIC ELWELL

HARVEST Kids™

HARVEST HOUSE PUBLISHERS
EUGENE, OREGON

A Fearless Leader

Text © 2018 by Rachel Spier Weaver and Anna Haggard
Artwork © 2018 by Eric Elwell

Published by Harvest House Publishers
Eugene, Oregon 97408

www.harvesthousepublishers.com

Published in association with the literary agency of Wolgemuth & Associates, Inc.

Cover and interior design by Left Coast Design

HARVEST KIDS is a registered trademark of The Hawkins Children's LLC. Harvest House Publishers, Inc., is the exclusive licensee of the federally registered trademark HARVEST KIDS.

ISBN 978-0-7369-7371-7 (hardcover)

Library of Congress Cataloging-in-Publication Data

Names: Weaver, Rachel Spier, author.
Title: A fearless leader: a Bible story about Deborah / Rachel Spier Weaver and Anna Haggard; illustrated by Eric Elwell.
Description: Eugene: Harvest House Publishers, 2018.
Identifiers: LCCN 2017060951 (print) | LCCN 2018005429 (ebook) | ISBN 9780736973724 (ebook) | ISBN 9780736973717 (hardcover)
Subjects: LCSH: Deborah (Biblical judge)—Juvenile literature.
Classification: LCC BS580.D4 (ebook) | LCC BS580.D4 W43 2018 (print) | DDC 222/.32092—dc23
LC record available at https://lccn.loc.gov/2017060951

Printed in China

18 19 20 21 22 23 24 25 26 / LP / 10 9 8 7 6 5 4 3 2 1

Deborah's Story
Judges 4–5

Based on the Old Testament story, *A Fearless Leader*
follows the biblical narrative of the heroine
Deborah, imagining how she responded
to the events recorded in Scripture.

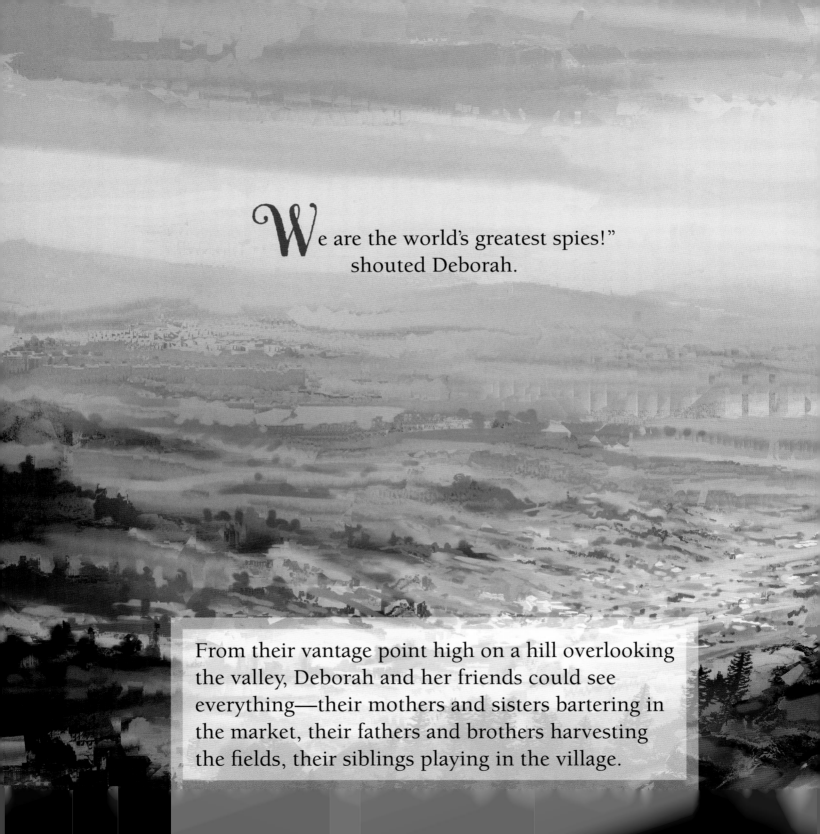

"We are the world's greatest spies!" shouted Deborah.

From their vantage point high on a hill overlooking the valley, Deborah and her friends could see everything—their mothers and sisters bartering in the market, their fathers and brothers harvesting the fields, their siblings playing in the village.

But no one could see them!

"Deborah, you have the best ideas," said one of her friends. Perceptive and imaginative, Deborah devised clever games, like spying on their parents!

"What's that?" asked another friend, pointing in the distance. The girls strained their eyes to see what looked like a swarm of bees overtaking the valley.

"Chariots! *Chariots!*" yelled Deborah.

Fear clutched her heart. King Jabin and his general, Sisera, were leading 900 horse-drawn chariots! Throughout the land of Israel, Sisera's chariots were dreaded for attacking towns. And they were headed to Deborah's village!

A friend screamed, "Run!"

Just when Deborah was about to bolt, she paused.
Who would alert the village to the danger?

But another thought gripped her. *If we take time to help the village, the chariots could catch us.*

In her heart, Deborah knew warning
the village was the right thing to do.

"We need to tell everyone about the chariots!"

Her friends hesitated. Then, bravely, they decided to follow Deborah.

They sped down the hill. "Sisera's chariots are here! Hide!" they yelled to everyone in the village.

Soon, Deborah's family and neighbors were dashing from their doorsteps to the ravines.

When they looked back at their homes, they saw
smoke rising. Sisera's army had pillaged the harvest.
They had stolen the sheep, cattle, and goats. And
they had set fire to the houses.

Nothing was left.

Deborah's family fled to the
hill country of Ephraim.

Meanwhile, Sisera continued to attack towns. To hide from him, families avoided the roads. They stopped celebrating holidays in the villages. And they were afraid to go outside at night.

They forgot how it felt to be free.

One day, Deborah sat under a palm tree that reached high above her head into the sky. "God, our people are scared. Would you free us from Jabin and Sisera?"

"One day, I will rescue my people," God whispered to Deborah's heart. "And Deborah, I have destined *you* to lead them to freedom."

Even though Deborah was young, God knew her heart was full of courage. For God had created Deborah and had called her to lead.

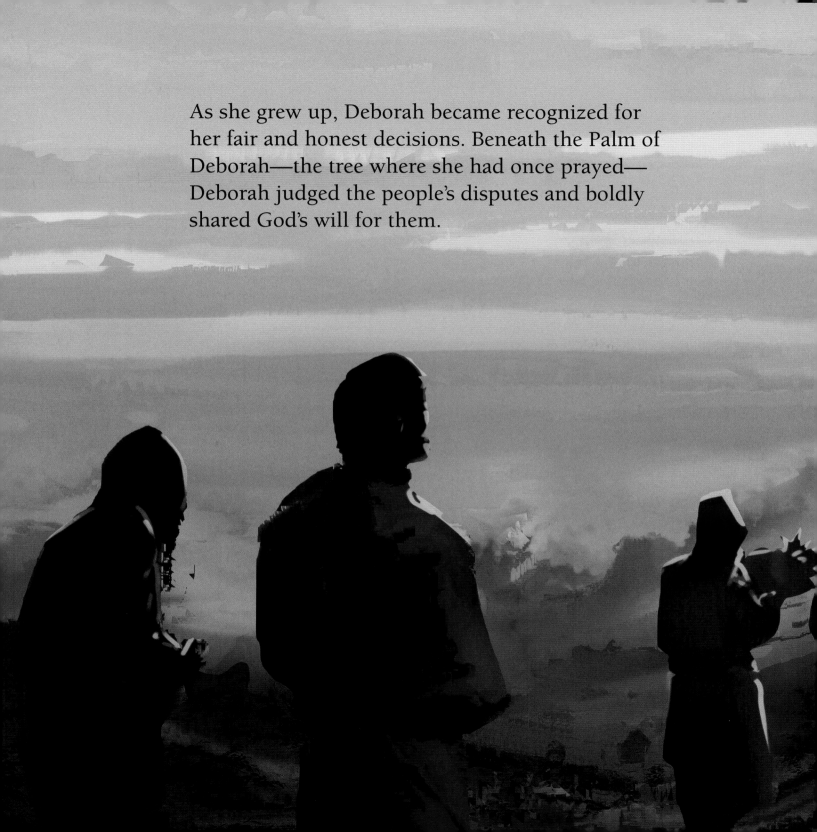

As she grew up, Deborah became recognized for her fair and honest decisions. Beneath the Palm of Deborah—the tree where she had once prayed—Deborah judged the people's disputes and boldly shared God's will for them.

Everyone trusted Deborah, and she became Israel's leader and prophet.

One day while she was sitting under the Palm of Deborah, God spoke.

"Deborah, now is the time to free my people!" Her heart soared. "Go and get Barak. Tell him to gather an army of 10,000 at Mount Tabor. There, by the Kishon River, I will save my people from Sisera's army."

Quickly, Deborah called Barak and shared God's message with him.

But Barak was afraid. "Deborah, Sisera has 900 chariots. Our people don't even own shields or spears. They're farmers! I'll go only if you go with me."

On their own, the Israelites could not defeat Sisera's chariots. But Barak had forgotten one thing: God was with the Israelites!

"Barak, I'll come with you," said Deborah. "But it isn't the size of an army, the speed of a chariot, or the strength of a general that wins battles.

"God alone gives us victory. Since you have not remembered that God is more powerful than Sisera, someone else will capture Sisera—a woman."

Throughout the countryside, Deborah and Barak asked their people to join the fight. "Freedom is ours. Follow us and see God bring us victory!"

Because the people loved Deborah and Barak, they listened to them. And 10,000 warriors trusted God and joined the battle!

They traveled up Mount Tabor, and there, Deborah, Barak, and the troops camped, waiting for Sisera

Suddenly, thousands of sleek warhorses pulling iron chariots came flying across the valley toward them. The warhorses' hooves pounded the earth. The chariots' wheels whirred. The commanders' whips snapped.

At that moment, Deborah remembered being a young girl watching Sisera's chariots charging toward her village.

Like then, she felt fear. But she knew the Creator of the earth would fight for them.

Heart pounding, Deborah turned to Barak. "Go! Today, God has delivered all of us from a stronger and fiercer enemy."

Just then, lighting struck the valley floor. Thunder rumbled as dark storm clouds appeared. And rain began to pour.

"Charge!" Barak bellowed, leading 10,000 men into battle.

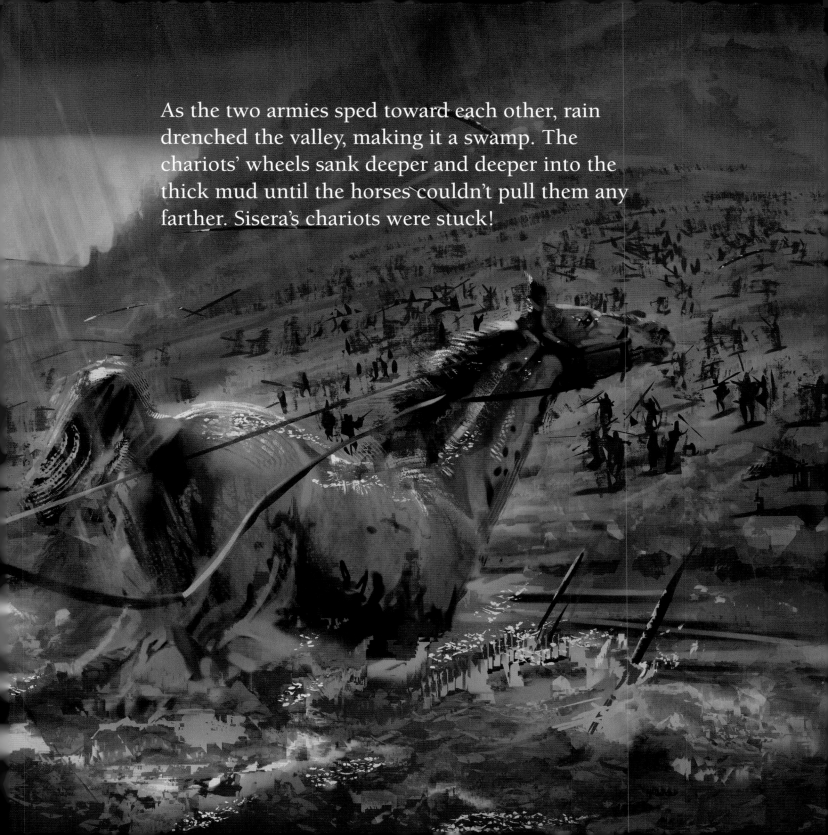

As the two armies sped toward each other, rain drenched the valley, making it a swamp. The chariots' wheels sank deeper and deeper into the thick mud until the horses couldn't pull them any farther. Sisera's chariots were stuck!

But the Israelites weren't burdened by chariots. With lighter weapons, they could outrun their enemy!

Watching from Mount Tabor, Deborah was ecstatic! She was witnessing God's rescue.

Then, *WHOOSH!*
Under the soaking rain, the Kishon River overflowed its banks, sweeping Sisera's mighty chariots downstream

God had provided the rain to trap them, giving the Israelites the chance to overtake their enemy!

But Sisera leaped from his own stuck chariot and began to sprint.

He ran…

and ran…

and ran.

He ran until he came to an old oak tree. And just as Deborah prophesied, Jael, a woman who lived in the tents nearby, captured him.

As the sun began to peek through the clouds, the
Israelite people ran from the mountains where
they had been hiding into the valley to celebrate
with Deborah and Barak.

They were free!

Deborah declared, "God has delivered us!"

The people were in awe—the fierce and mighty chariots were no match against their God!

God loved Deborah and had specially chosen her to lead the people to freedom. Looking up at the bright sky, Deborah thanked God for fulfilling the promise to rescue them.

Then she sang for joy. "May all your enemies fall like Sisera, God. But may everyone who loves you become like the sun rising high and strong."

- Deborah showed great bravery when she warned her family and friends about a dangerous situation. We show bravery when we do things like telling the truth even when it is hard or standing up to someone who is hurting others' feelings. What have you done that was brave?

- God created Deborah to be courageous and wise and to lead the Israelites. She made good decisions and shared God's will with her people. What types of traits has God given you? Your parents and grandparents may have ideas to share too!

- In the story, Barak and the Israelites were scared of Sisera's chariots. But God rescued the people from the mighty chariots. What are you afraid of? Pray and ask God to help you remember that you don't need to be afraid, for God is always with you.

Dear reader,

What Bible stories captured your attention as a child? The stories dramatized on Sunday school felt boards often featured Noah and his ark, David and Goliath, and Paul traveling on his missionary journeys. And rightly so! These stories depict giants of our faith. But the Bible also elevates women—faith-filled adventurers who lead, make brave decisions, and risk everything to follow God. Called and Courageous Girls is a series of children's books that star gutsy biblical women who unleash the kingdom of God.

We are thrilled that you have chosen to read this book in the Called and Courageous Girls series. Our prayer is that these books will provide hours of enjoyable reading, prompt engaging and challenging conversations, and inspire your children to use their talents, passions, and gifts for the kingdom.

Blessings,

Rachel and Anna